T0145167

SOOL OF A KING

Martial Yapo

To order additional copies of this book, contact:
Xlibris
844-714-8691
www.Xlibris.com
Orders@Xlibris.com

ISBN: Softcover   978-1-6641-9182-2
        Hardcover   978-1-5434-9771-7
        EBook   978-1-6641-9181-5

Print information available on the last page

Rev. date: 05/19/2022

Bonjour! This means "Hi" in French!
I'm Kingston Olivier Yapo, but you can call me King!

Let me tell you a little about my story:

The first thing you need to know is that I'm a lefty. My parents tell me that alone makes me special! I'm an artist and a soccer player.

My Papa always says "Football, King! It's Football!" Not really, but OK, Papa!

These are my parents. My Maman is from California. She is tall and blonde with big, beautiful blue eyes. My Papa is African-French. He is very proud of his roots and he is very tall. We are a great team.

My parents are fun! They like to spend time together, listening to music, often without me.

Now that I think about it, maybe *not* the best *team* spirit… hmmm.

Maman and Papa always talk about music and fashion. They tell me

"King, just watch and listen, follow the process!" They say there are so many good things out there I still have to learn about. I don't know about that… because I do know a lot about music, art and other stuff. We are *always* debating about what I still have left to learn.

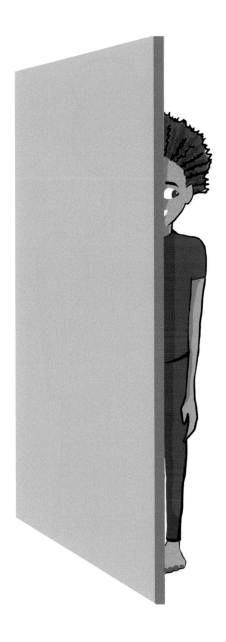

Oh! Actually, we are four! Let me introduce you to my brother!

I have a big brother named Soolshyne. He lives in the stars. I never had the chance to meet him, but my parents say his spirit is with us every day, and I believe them.

Sometimes I try to talk to him during my sleep but he never talks back to me. I wish he would be here with me to play and watch movies.

I am so playful, especially right before bed, like all 6-year-old kids! My maman and papa don't like when I'm playful at bedtime. Sometimes I get in trouble for this.

Kingston!!!
It is time to go to bed now, baby boy!

I always have to remind them that this is what kids do, so I'm doing what I'm supposed to do, right? But they don't understand my arguments, or they don't want to understand them, especially at bedtime!

Going to bed is the worst moment of my life!
But my parents say that is just the reality of a kid's life!
Brush your teeth.
Put on your jammies.
It's not that fun.

Meanwhile, the parents are downstairs, chilling, laughing, cooking and watching movies.

It doesn't seem like a fair deal to me, don't you agree? It's not fair.

... And by the way, look; I'm not even tired! What does it even mean, "being tired?"

I feel like adults make up things just for us kids to fall into theirs traps.

Do I look like I'm tired! Look at my eyes! Hey!! Look! Wide open!!

- Wait... What...
  Soolshyne!!! What are you doing here brother!!!!?
  Am I dreaming!? What's happening?

- Bonjour Kingston,
  No, you are not dreaming, I mean not completely. This is your reality,
  but nobody can see us.

Woooah! That's really cool! You have magical powers!

So, Papa and Maman were right when they told me you would appear in my dreams. They said you would, but that was a long time ago and you didn't come, and I thought they were just making it up or something.

What were you doing brother? I've been waiting for you all of my life!

- I know, I'll explain it all to you. Come with me, I'm going to help you get ready for school. We have so much catching up to do, Lil brother.

First of all, I'm so happy to be here with you. We Angels can't appear in a human's life just because it's what we want. We have to respect the process of life and allow things to happen in their own time.

You guys need to do the work to reach out to us and open the door to your inner self.

- But Papa has been ready, Soolshyne. He misses you so much, you don't want to see him? Don't you miss your mom too?
- I would love to see them Kingston, but it is not that simple. I visit my mom pretty often, as well as Papa. But his life journey took a turn that doesn't include me physically. I'm always with him in his spirit. He knows that.
- I see
- But it is why you've been sent here, to feel his heart of love and hope. You did a great job!
- That's funny he always says those exact words
- I know I've been with you all the time Lil man!
- No, you weren't!

- They told you that when you were a baby you were laughing like nobody's business right? Alone, in your bed?
- Yeah, I heard that a lot
- Who do you think was entertaining you?
- You did????
- Yeah boy!
- Well, I can have fun on my own too, you know!
- Oh boy!

- Also, do you think there are many babies who start walking at 8 months old.
- Wait … Papa told me, it's a Yapo thing!
- Duh…He doesn't know anything about that, adults always think they know it all! I was holding your hands. I was your flesh and bones, directly connected to your soul.

- And … when you biked for the first time… I was there too, making that bike stand up, when you were about to fall hard on the ground. I've been here all the time.
- Ok. Get yourself ready for school… I will see you there.
- What! You are coming to school? So cool!
- I will be hanging out with you…

- Stop talking and listen to the teacher.
- Are you for real right now, so you're going to show up to police me like that?
- Yep!
- Kingston! Why are you talking to yourself? Are you ok?
- Yeah, yeah, yeah, I'm so great right now, I'm doing great! ... Terrific!

- Aaaaah! Look at Kingston Is wearing a pink t-shirt, like a girl!
- If somebody doesn't stop me right now, I'm going to lose my temper…
- That kid is literally wearing khaki shorts and he's laughing at me? Really?
- Ok, Lil brother, you need to calm down, stay Zen. I'm the voice you need to listen right now, not the other one!
- I can't… I can't do that… I'm furious!
- Breathe!!!!

After spending days together, Kingston's parents noticed a change in his behavior. Something had changed. He was still a joyful child, maybe even more than before. But he suddenly became much more independent, playing on his own, going to bed early without arguing. Maman and Papa didn't understand, but deep in their hearts they knew.

- Thank you for being here for me, Sool.
- I waited for this moment a long time, thank you for including me in your life.
- So, are you going to stay with me forever?
- Unfortunately, I can't stay forever.
- But you just got here. C'mon, stay a little bit longer.
- Part of the reason I came was to teach you the agreements of life. Now that you know them, I have to go back. But I'm going to make sure you stay in line, though.
- Ok! I can do that...
- So, you are going back to the stars? What is life about there?
- Like you would imagine, full of love and kindness.
- That's all? Just love and kindness? Nothing else?
- Yeah what else do you need?
- I don't know...Toys? Candies? And more???
- Love and kindness are all you need!

- Can I ask you a big favor before you leave?
- Yes what?
- Dude, I mean… you have wings, can you fly me around?
- Ohhhh… I don't know if I can do that. I mean…not sure I can… I guess I can…

Ooooh boy!

Wooooo!!!
Papa and Maman are always telling me that I'm living my best life, but they have no idea how great my life is right now!!! ... wooooo!!!

- Ok little brother it's time for me to go.
- I know, thank you for everything big brother, I will be a good boy and listen to my parents and give the best version of myself every day. You can count on me.

- I know you will, and I will come when it is time for me to be here.
- Please come to see me soon, and then we can play Legos or something. Maybe we can watch a movie, ok?

- Ok King!

- I'm feeling sad, Soolshyne. I wish you could be here with me. Life with a big brother is so much better.

- Feeling sad is a natural feeling, I am sad to leave but these are tears of joy, 'cause I'm so proud of you for who you are becoming.

Fly Angel, say Hi to the family up there,

My brother has returned.

Kingston's life took a turn for the better. What he had been wishing for during the six years of his young life happened because he was in tune with his inner self.